Violin / Book 3

The ABC's of Violin
for the
Advanced
Book 3

by

Janice Tucker Rhoda

For more information about *The ABC's of Strings* visit
www.abcsofstrings.com

CARL FISCHER®
65 Bleecker Street, New York, NY 10012

Copyright © 1998, 2003 by Janice Tucker Rhoda
International Copyright Secured.
All rights reserved including performing rights.
WARNING! This publication is protected by Copyright law. To photocopy or reproduce by
any method is an infringement of the Copyright law. Anyone who reproduces copyrighted
matter is subject to substantial penalties and assessments for each infringement.
Printed in the U.S.A.

ABC5

ISBN 0-9663731-3-8

PREFACE

This violin method book is designed for the more advanced student of any age. After many years of combining various methods of teaching both children and adults, I have developed a simple and enjoyable approach for the study of the violin. I use materials which help students advance technically in a gradual, logical and thorough manner. There are short, lyrical warm-up exercises and longer study pieces, as well as familiar classical and popular melodies. I composed seventeen of the thirty-seven, which fit in perfectly with the development of left-hand and bowing techniques.

To the adult student: I am convinced that it is never too late to begin studying the violin. In fact, adult beginners learn to read music at a very quick pace, have excellent concentration and are highly motivated to practice. Playing the violin is very engaging and the contents of this book are sure to maintain your continued interest.

To the teacher: During my many years of teaching and directing string departments, I dreamed of developing a method that would help beginners of any age feel more at ease and satisfied – a method that would allow them to progress quickly and play precisely, yet learn to read music well. This method book, and the entire series, is designed to fit these criteria.

Here are some key elements to strive for at a lesson:

1. impeccable intonation
2. solid bow technique
3. correct posture
4. steady rhythm
5. accurate reading
6. beautiful tone quality
7. expressive vibrato
8. structured, artistic phrasing
9. precise shifting
10. memorization of pieces*

In any case, it is wise to help our students develop good habits right from the start.

Teaching students of all ages is very gratifying. I think teachers will have the same positive experience I have had while using the series.

— Janice Tucker Rhoda
New England Conservatory of Music Faculty and Alumna

* Although it is not essential to memorize pieces, as a teacher I have found it to be a very useful tool in developing a student's skill. To paraphrase Rudolf Kolisch (1896-1978), a good memory is a habit formed. His quartet, the Kolisch String Quartet, was the first to perform its works by memory.

I dedicate this book to my devoted teachers:

Nancy Cirillo, Alan Hawryluk, Joseph Leary, Rudolf Kolisch,
Yuri Mazurkevich, George Neikrug, Daniel Pinkham, Eric Rosenblith,
Gunther Schuller, Roman Totenberg, and Benjamin Zander.

TABLE OF CONTENTS
(Excludes warm-ups)

TITLE	COMPOSER	PAGE
España	J.T. Rhoda	1
This Land Is Your Land	Woody Guthrie	2
Reuben And Rachel	English Folk Song	3
Good Night Ladies	American Folk Song	3
Trill Study No. 1,2,3	J.T. Rhoda	4-5
Watching the Train Go By	J.T. Rhoda	5
Bach Meditation	J.T. Rhoda	6
Courante Study	J.T. Rhoda	7
Young Mozart	J.T. Rhoda	8
First Nowell	English Carol	9
Gregorian Chant	J.T. Rhoda	9
Longing for the Russian Homeland	J.T. Rhoda	10
Symphony No. 40	W.A. Mozart	10
The Singing Strad	J.T. Rhoda	11
Sur Le Pont D'Avignon	French Folk Song	12
George Washington	J.T. Rhoda	12
Oh Dear, What Can the Matter Be	Scottish Folk Song	13
Old Folks At Home	Stephen Foster	14
Home Sweet Home	American Folk Song	14
Everything's Coming Up Roses	J.T. Rhoda	16
Fiddler's Holiday	J.T. Rhoda	16

THIRD POSITION

Swinging High!	J.T. Rhoda	18
This Old Man	American Folk Song	21
Strolling Through the Park	J.T. Rhoda	22
The King's Jester	J.T. Rhoda	22
Annie Laurie	English Folk Song	24
Scarborough Fair	English Folk Song	25
Rondeau	Jean Joseph Mouret	25
Michael, Row The Boat Ashore	American Folk Song	27
The Riddle Song	American Folk Song	27
The More We Get Together (*Ach, Du Lieber Augustin!*)	German Folk Song	28
Over The River and Through the Woods	American Folk Song	28
School Time	J.T. Rhoda	29
Waltzing Matilda	Marie Cowan	29
The Streets of Laredo	American Folk Song	30
Yellow Rose of Texas	American Folk Song	31
Baroque Study No. 1	J.T. Rhoda	33
Scales and Arpeggios		35
Worksheet		39
Staff Paper		40
Practice Chart		41
Practice Planner		43

LESSON 1
SPICCATO

① Warm-ups

②

C means Common time (4/4)

España

J. T. Rhoda

③ Allegretto ♩ = 110–120

Count: 1 2 3 + 4 +   1 2 + 3 + 4 +

Fine

Be sure to look for the Easy Piano Accompaniment for Book 3.

D.C. al fine

Page 1

This Land Is Your Land

Words and Music by
Woody Guthrie

④ Moderato

Jan 19

LESSON 2
4TH FINGER C ON THE E STRING

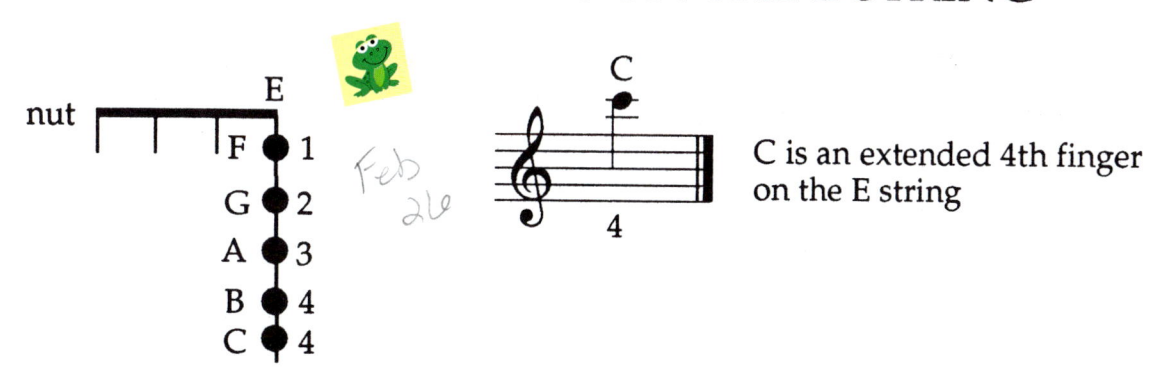

C is an extended 4th finger on the E string

Feb 26

⑤ Warm-ups

⑥

Reuben And Rachel
English Folk Song

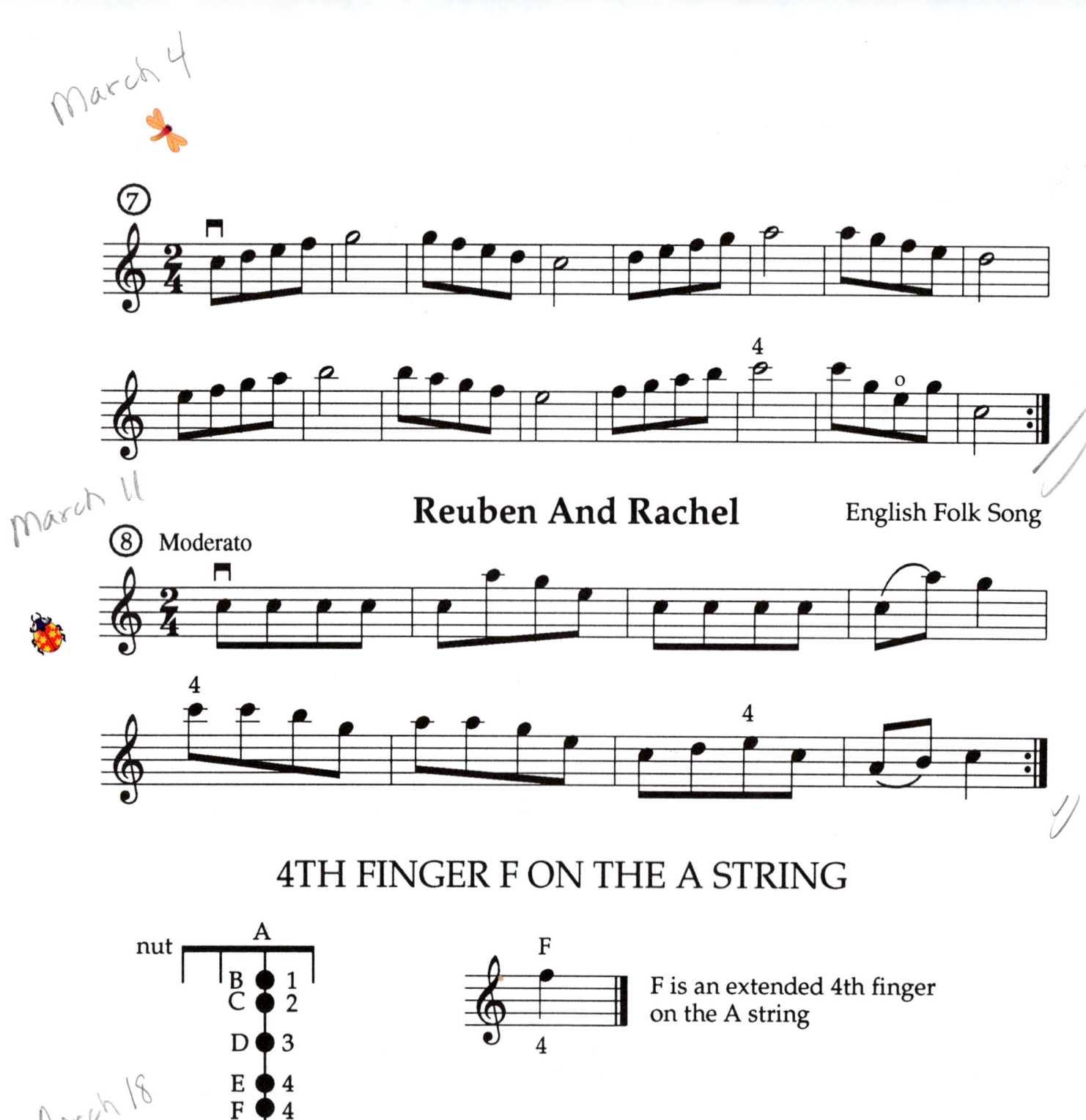

⑧ Moderato

4TH FINGER F ON THE A STRING

F is an extended 4th finger on the A string

⑨ Warm-up

Good Night Ladies
American Folk Song

⑩ Moderato

spiccato

Page 3

LESSON 3
Trill Study No. 1

J. T. Rhoda

> is an accent sign. Accent the note with the bow.

tr means trill. A trill is an ornament that consists of two notes which alternate rapidly. The printed note alternates with the note above in the existing key.

April 8th

♪ is a thirtysecond note. Rhythmic equations: 𝅘𝅥𝅰𝅘𝅥𝅰 = 𝅘𝅥𝅯𝅘𝅥𝅯 = 𝅘𝅥𝅮 and 𝅘𝅥𝅰𝅘𝅥𝅰𝅘𝅥𝅰𝅘𝅥𝅰 = 𝅘𝅥𝅮

Trill Study No. 2

⑫ ♪ = 50-80   Count the rhythm aloud before playing!

J. T. Rhoda

* 1 e + a   2 e + a   3 e + a   4 +

* say: "one ee and ah"

April 15

Trill Study No. 3

⑬ ♩ = 69-88

J. T. Rhoda

Watching The Train Go By

⑭ Allegro ♩ = 138

J. T. Rhoda

spiccato

Page 5

LESSON 4
A Harmonic Minor Scale

*optional: Use a continuous vibrato on each note.

Bach Meditation

Andante ♩ = 80

J. T. Rhoda

espressivo

rit.

Courante Study

⑰ ♩ = 80 -108

J. T. Rhoda

< is a crescendo sign (gradually louder)

> is a decrescendo sign (gradually softer)

LESSON 5
B♭ ON THE E STRING

B♭ is low 4th finger on the E string

⑱ Warm-up

Young Mozart

⑲ Allegretto ♩ = 116

J. T. Rhoda

poco rit.

First Nowell

Andante — (20)

English Carol

rit.

G Harmonic Minor Scale

(21)

6 means 6 beats per measure.
4 means a quarter note receives 1 beat.

Gregorian Chant

(22) Andante ♩ = 80

J. T. Rhoda

1 2 3 4 5 6

poco rit.

Page 9

Longing For The Russian Homeland

J. T. Rhoda

(23) Adagio ♩ = 60

mf espressivo

p

mf rubato ... *molto rit.*

(24) Warm-up

Symphony No. 40
1st movement

Wolfgang Amadeus Mozart

(25) Allegro molto

2da volta *poco rit.*

Page 10

LESSON 6
A♭ ON THE D STRING

Sur Le Pont D'Avignon
On The Bridge of Avignon

(29) Moderato — French Folk Song

George Washington

(30) Allegretto ♩ = 69 — J. T. Rhoda

1st verse: George Wash-ing-ton, a cher-ry tree, he chopped it down says his-to-ry. He
*2nd verse
told the truth in spite of shame. He could not lie, he took the blame!

meno mosso ♩ = 60

Refrain: George Wash-ing-ton a man of hon-or was our pres-i-dent. His
for-ti-tude and true de-vo-tion made us con-fi-dent. A
lead-er strong in war and peace he set our na-tion free. The
found-ing fa-ther of our land he gave us lib-er-ty.

*2nd verse: George Washington, a young man true
Became a soldier when he grew.
With many braves ones by his side
He won the battles far and wide.

poco rit.

Page 12

LESSON 7

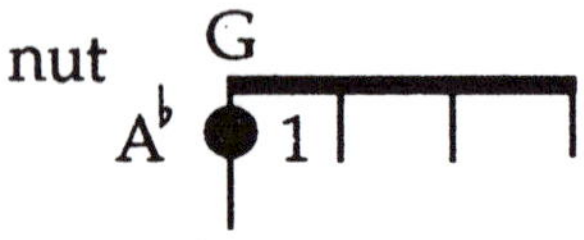

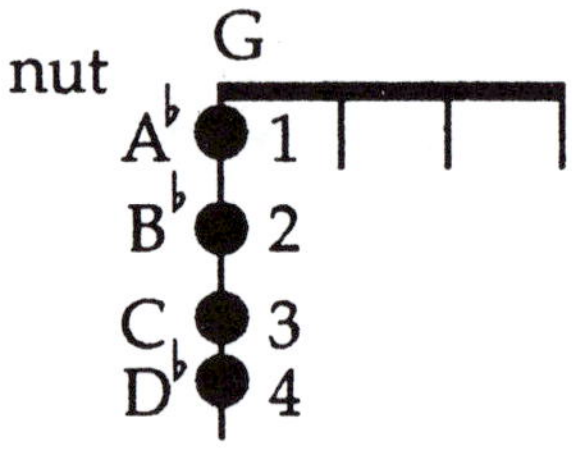

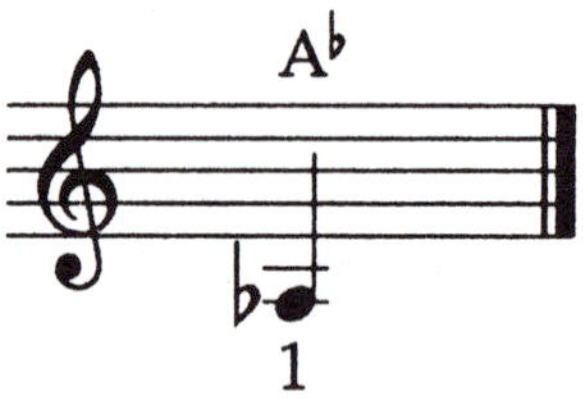

A♭ is low 1st finger on the G string

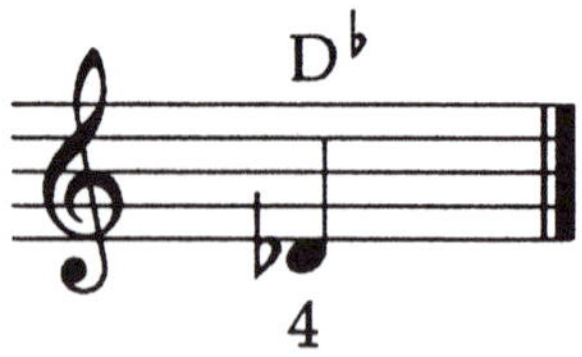

D♭ is low 4th finger on the G string

㉛ Warm-ups

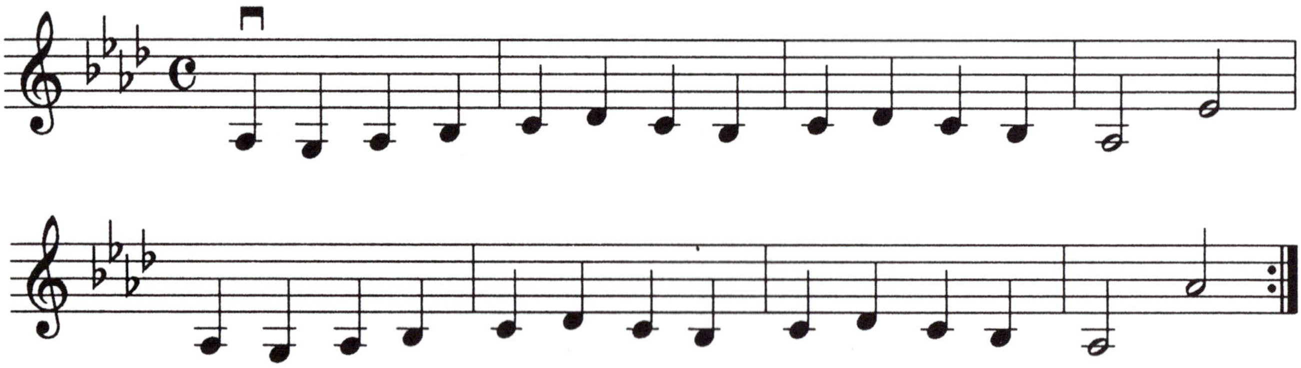

㉜

㉝

Oh Dear, What Can The Matter Be

㉞ Moderato

Scottish Folk Song

Old Folks At Home

(35) Andante
Stephen Foster

mf espressivo   1 2 3 +4

f   (♭)

mf   *poco rit.*

Home Sweet Home

(36) Andantino
American Folk Song

mp dolce

mf

poco rit.

LESSON 8
Double Stops

Place the bow on Open A string and Open E string at the same time.

37. Warm-ups

Learn to check an octave

3 means 3 beats per measure.
8 means an eighth note receives 1 beat.

Everything's Coming Up Roses

50 Allegro vivace ♪ = 152-184

J. T. Rhoda

spiccato

Fiddler's Holiday

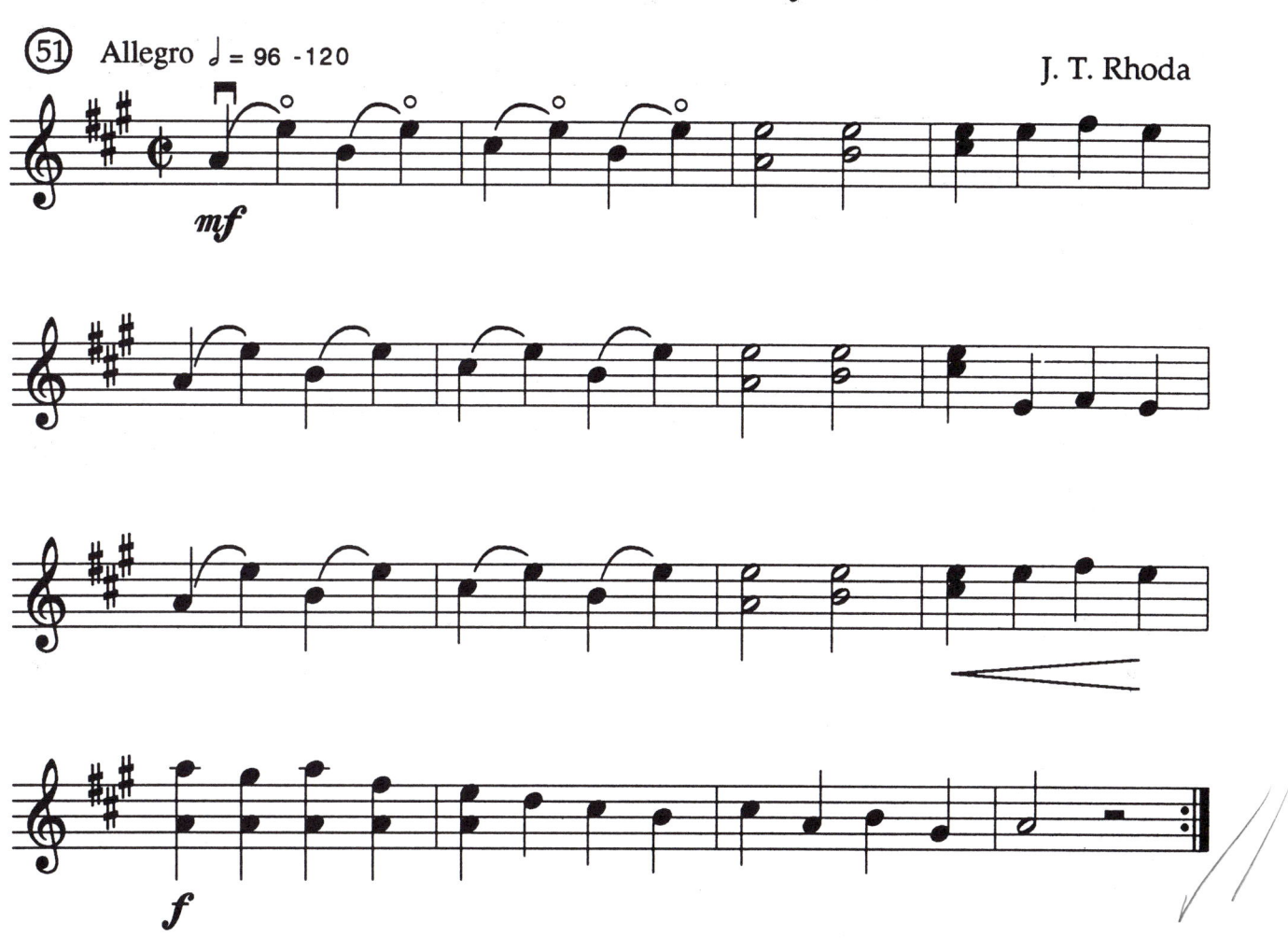

51 Allegro ♩ = 96 -120

J. T. Rhoda

mf

f

Page 16

THIRD POSITION
LESSON 9
Third Position On The A String

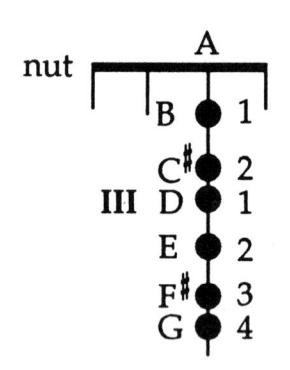

D E F#G in third position on the A string

Roman Numeral **I** means first position.
Roman Numeral **III** means third position.

52 Warm-ups

* shift

III ** restez

* Shift the left hand to third position.
** Restez means stay in the position.

53

54

Page 17

Swinging High!

Moderato ♩ = 100

J. T. Rhoda

Now I go mer-ri-ly swing-ing on the swing! Up so high eas-i-ly reach-ing to the sky!

Shifting Exercises

LESSON 10
Third Position On The E String

Feb 19

A B C# D in third position on the E string

65 Warm-ups

66

67

Page 20

*D Major Scale In Third Position

*D Major 2 octave scale: page 35

⑦⓪ Warm-ups

This Old Man

⑦② Moderato

American Folk Song

Strolling Through The Park

(73) Andante ♩ = 88

J. T. Rhoda

The King's Jester

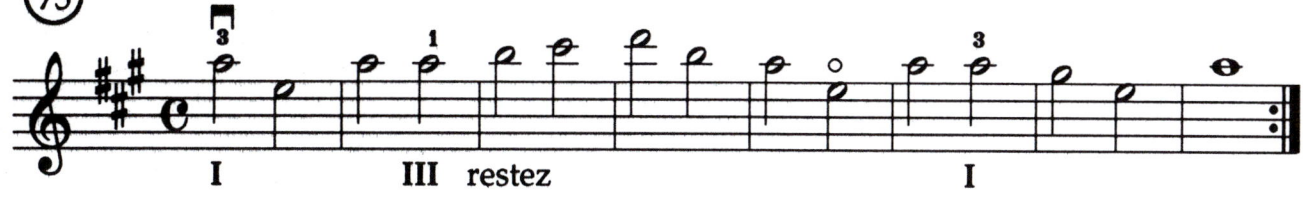

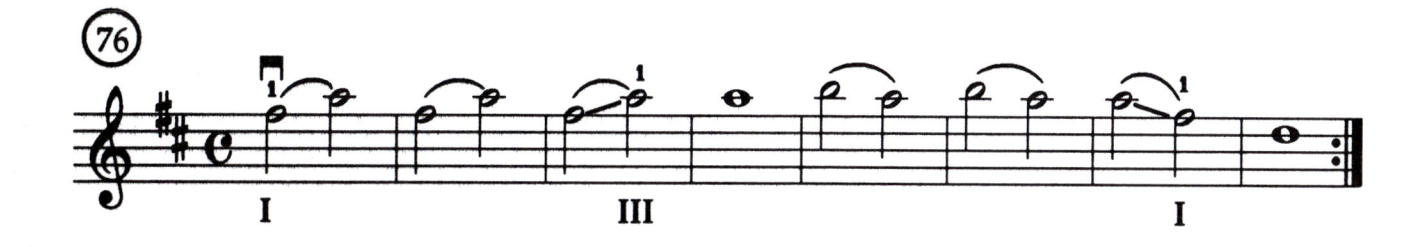

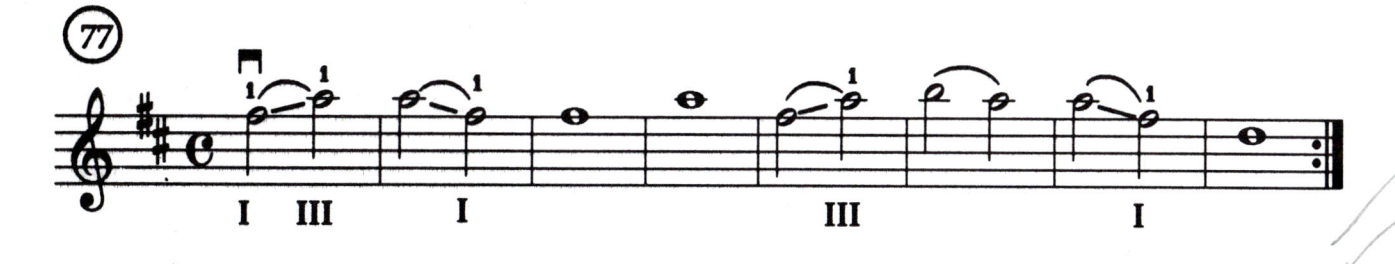

(74) Andantino ♩ = 100

J. T. Rhoda

III restez

Shifting Exercises

(75)

I   III restez   I

(76)

I   III   I

(77)

I III   I   III   I

LESSON 11
Third Position On The D String

G A B C in third position on the D string

⑦⑧ Warm-ups

⑦⑨

* G Major Scale In Third Position

⑧⓪

*G Major 2 octave scale: page 35

⑧①

⑧② III restez

⑧③ III restez

Page 23

Annie Laurie

English Folk Song

(84) Larghetto

espressivo

poco rit.

Shifting Exercises

(85)

(86)

(87)

(88) Warm-up

Page 24

Scarborough Fair

English Folk Song

LESSON 12
Third Position On The G String

C Major Scale In Third Position

* C Major 2 octave scale: page 36

Page 26

Michael, Row The Boat Ashore

(97) Moderato — American Folk Song

Shifting Exercises

(98)

(99)

The Riddle Song

(100) Allegretto — American Folk Song

The More We Get Together
Ach, Du Lieber Augustin!

German Folk Song

Over The River And Through The Woods

American Folk Song

School Time

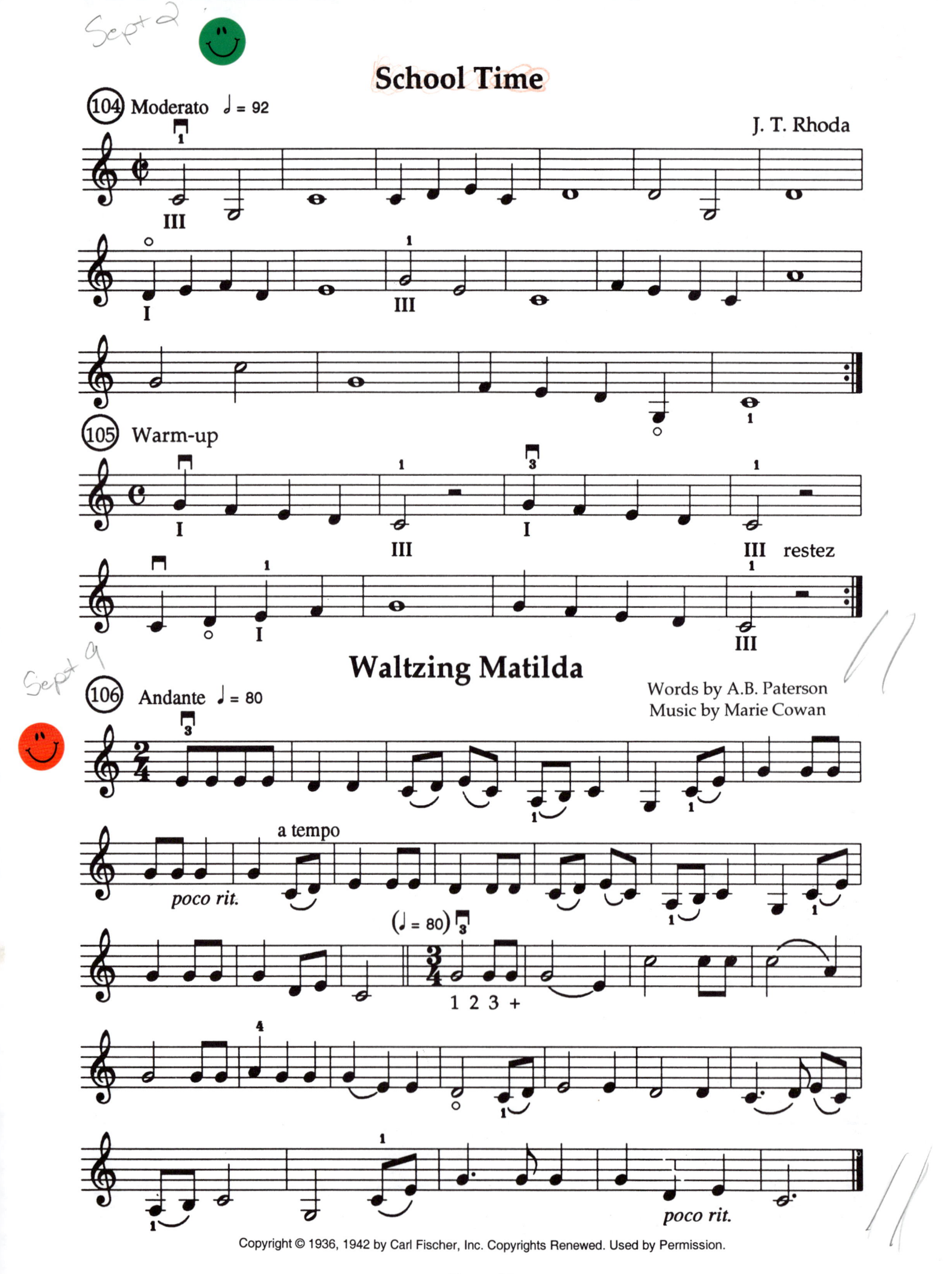

J. T. Rhoda

(104) Moderato ♩ = 92

(105) Warm-up

Waltzing Matilda

Words by A.B. Paterson
Music by Marie Cowan

(106) Andante ♩ = 80

poco rit. *a tempo*

(♩ = 80)

poco rit.

Copyright © 1936, 1942 by Carl Fischer, Inc. Copyrights Renewed. Used by Permission.

Page 29

LESSON 13

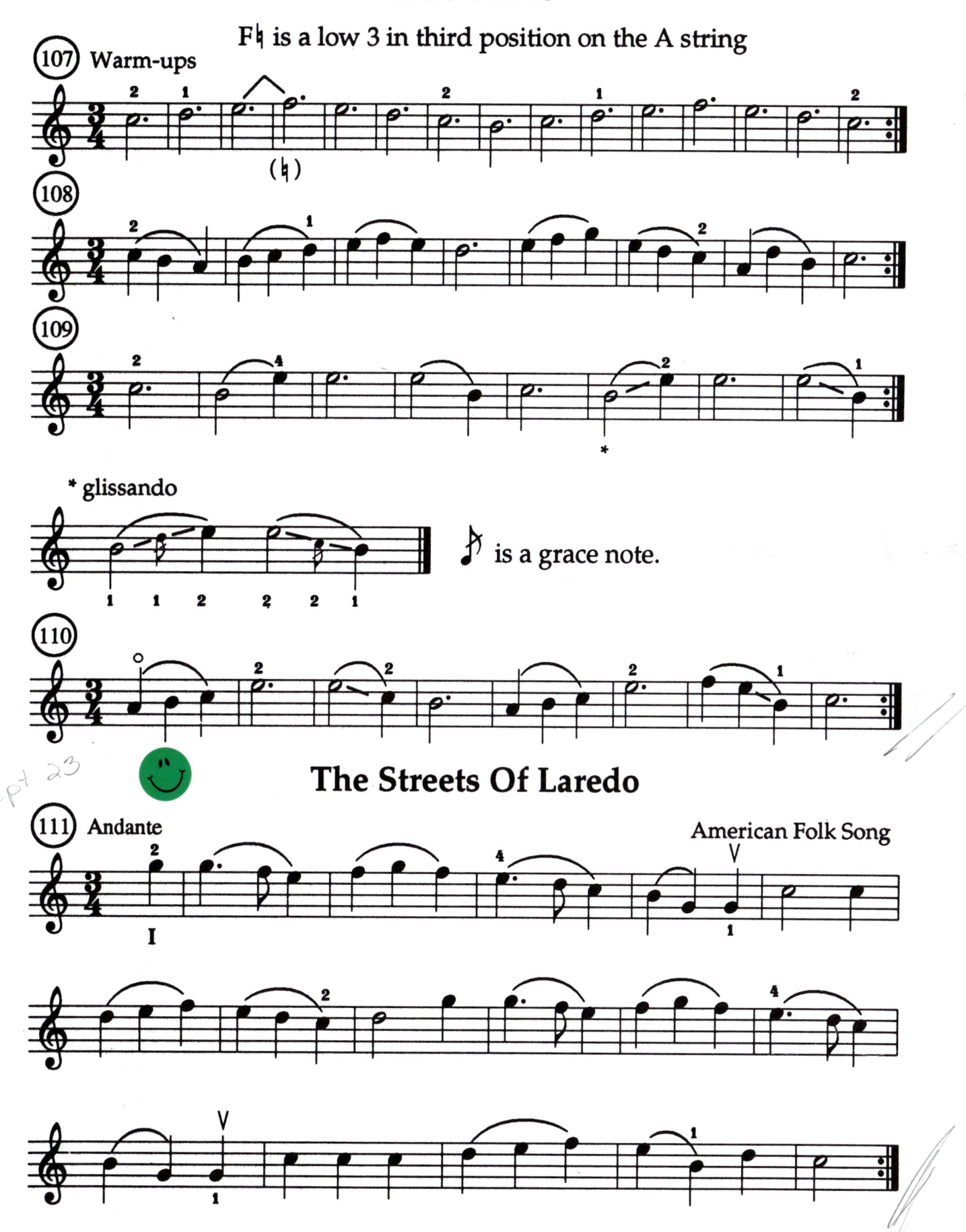

F♮ is a low 3 in third position on the A string

(107) Warm-ups

(108)

(109)

glissando

♪ is a grace note.

(110)

The Streets Of Laredo

(111) Andante — American Folk Song

Yellow Rose Of Texas

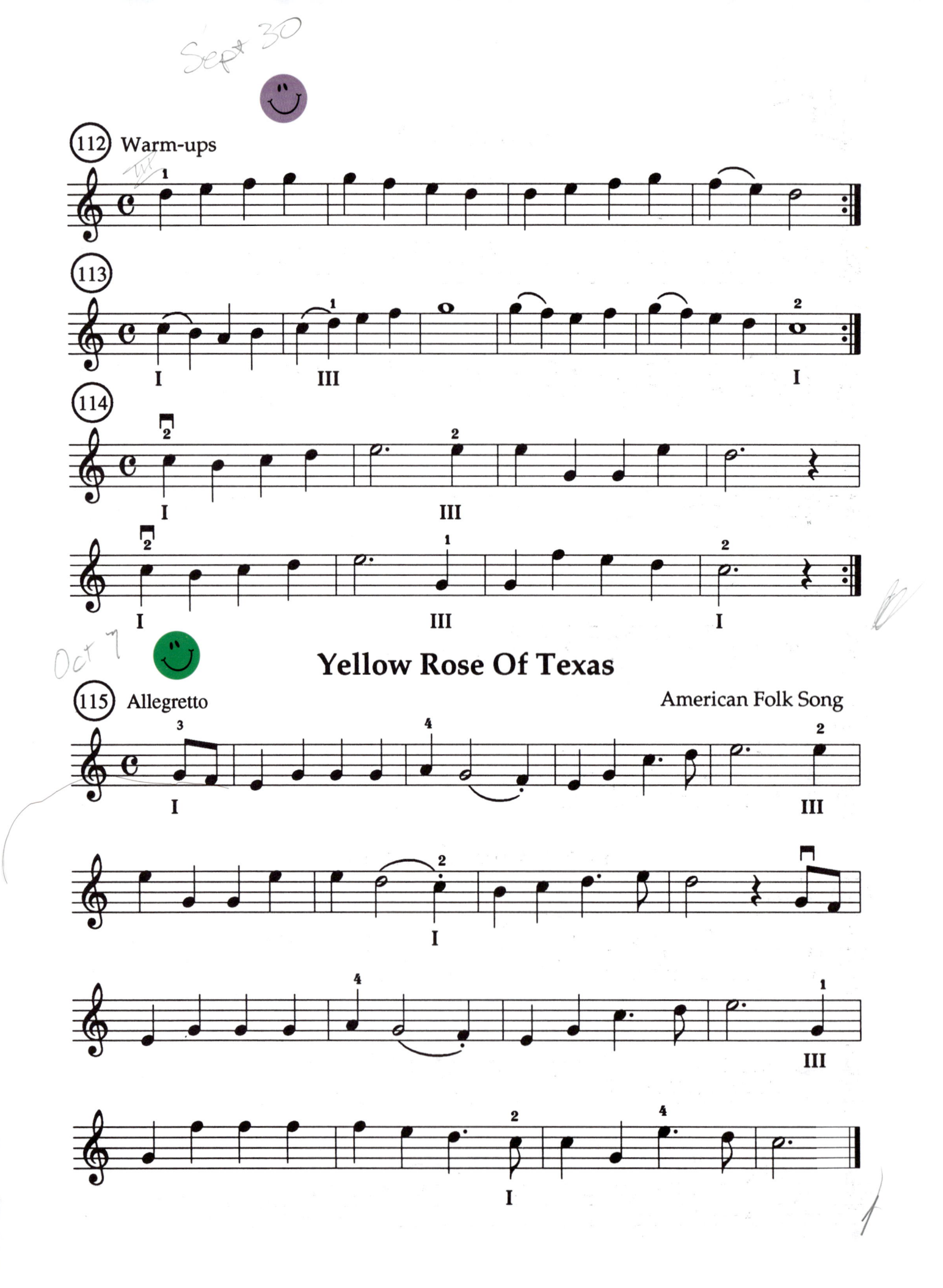

American Folk Song

Allegretto

LESSON 14
C♮ is a low 3 in third position on the E string

Baroque Study No. 1

J. T. Rhoda

Page 34

LESSON 15
9 MAJOR SCALES AND 9 ARPEGGIOS

E MAJOR

C MAJOR

F MAJOR

B♭ MAJOR

E♭ MAJOR

A♭ MAJOR

LESSON 16
4 NATURAL MINOR SCALES AND 4 ARPEGGIOS

A MINOR

D MINOR

G MINOR

E MINOR

Use your metronome at different speeds: ♩ = 50 ♩ = 60 ♩ = 80

Use varied rhythms:

Use varied bowings:

Worksheet

Directions:
1. Write the letter names above the notes.
2. Write the finger numbers below the notes.

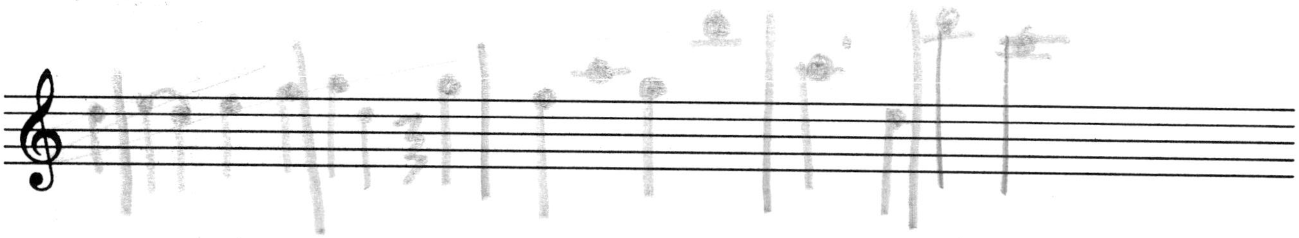

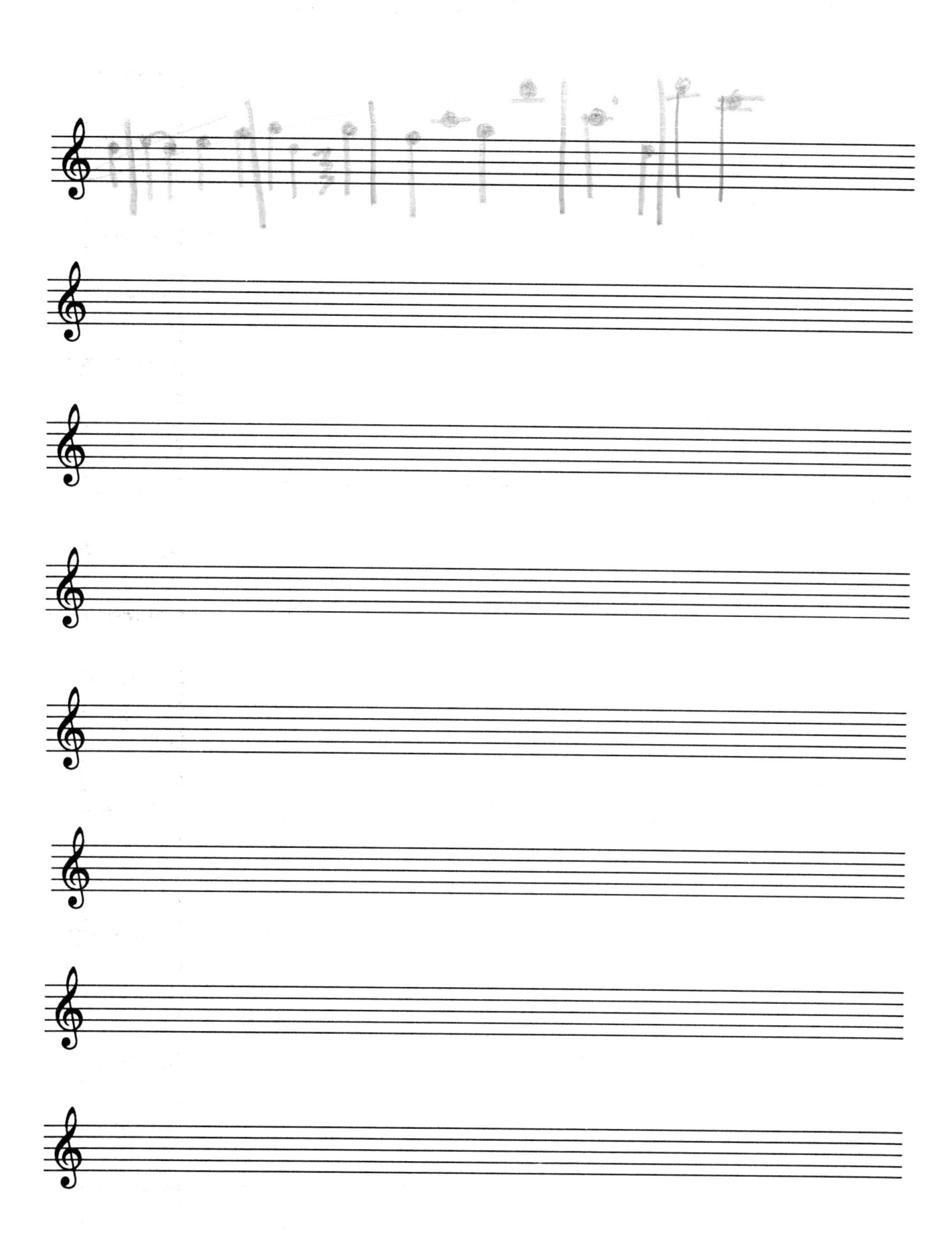

_____'s ABCs Practice Chart
Age____

Lesson Day Date									Practiced This Week	Stars
	Lesson counts: 30 min.								25 min.	★
	Lesson counts: 30 min.								25 min.	★
	Lesson counts: 30 min.								25 min.	★
	Lesson counts: 30 min.								25 min.	★
	Lesson counts: 30 min.								25 min.	
	Lesson counts: 30 min.								25 min.	
	Lesson counts: 30 min.								25 min.	★
	Lesson counts: 30 min.								25 min.	★
	Lesson counts: 30 min.								25 min.	★
	Lesson counts: 30 min.								25 min.	★
	Lesson counts: 30 min.								25 min.	★
	Lesson counts: 30 min.								25 min.	★
	Lesson counts: 30 min.								25 min.	★
	Lesson counts: 30 min.								25 min.	★
	Lesson counts: 30								25 min.	★
	Lesson counts: 30 min.								25 min.	★
	Lesson counts: 30 min.								25 min.	★
	Lesson counts: 30 min.								25 min.	★

ABC5

Please Practice Every Day

_____'s ABCs Practice Chart
Age____

Lesson-Day Date								Practiced This Week	Stars
	Lesson counts: min.							min.	
	Lesson counts: min.							min.	
	Lesson counts: min.							min.	
	Lesson counts: min.							min.	
	Lesson counts: min.							min.	
	Lesson counts: min.							min.	
	Lesson counts: min.							min.	
	Lesson counts: min.							min.	
	Lesson counts: min.							min.	
	Lesson counts: min.							min.	
	Lesson counts: min.							min.	
	Lesson counts: min.							min.	
	Lesson counts: min.							min.	
	Lesson counts: min.							min.	
	Lesson counts: min.							min.	
	Lesson counts: min.							min.	
	Lesson counts: min.							min.	
	Lesson counts: min.							min.	

ABC5

Please Practice Every Day

PRACTICE PLANNER

DATE	PAGE	GOALS/COMMENTS	REMARKS

ABC5

The ABC's of Strings
by Janice Tucker Rhoda

What they're saying about the ABCs of Strings Series:

"The best string method books I've seen in years!"
— Yuri Mazurkevich: Professor of Violin, Boston University

"The perfect tool with its simple melodies appropriate for adults as well as children."
— Meredith Cooper: Violin/Viola Teacher, Boston Center for Adult Education

"The ABCs ... are a truly valuable resource for every teacher of students in the early stages of exploring the instrument."
— Dorothy DeLay: Professor of Violin, The Juilliard School

A Complete Series of Method Books

Instrument Books and Catalog Numbers	Violin	Viola	Cello	Bass
Book 1 – Absolute Beginner	ABC1	ABC7	ABC13	ABC25 For Beginning to Intermediate
Performance & Play-Along CD	ABC1^{CD}			
Book 2 – Intermediate	ABC3	ABC9	ABC15	ABC27 For the Developing Student
Book 3 – Advanced	ABC5	ABC11	ABC17	
Book 4 – More Advanced	ABC19			
Book 5 – Budding Virtuoso	ABC21			

Easy Piano Accompaniments for	Violin	Viola	Cello	Bass
Book 1 – Absolute Beginner	ABC2	ABC8	ABC14	ABC26
Book 2 – Intermediate	ABC4	ABC10	ABC16	ABC28
Book 3 – Advanced	ABC6	ABC12	ABC18	
Book 4 – More Advanced	ABC20			
Book 5 – Budding Virtuoso	ABC22			

The ABC's of Duets
Multi-level Duet Book

Two Violins	ABC23

The ABC's of String Orchestra
A Beginning Ensemble Folio

Ensemble Books and Instrumentation	Cat. No.
Full Score	ABC101
Violin I	ABC102
Violin II	ABC103
Viola	ABC104
Cello	ABC105
Bass	ABC106
Piano Accompaniment	ABC107

ISBN 0-9663731-3-8

The ABC's of Strings
CARL FISCHER®
65 Bleecker Street, New York, NY 10012
www.carlfischer.com
ABC5 — $8.95 USA